The ABC of INTENTIONAL SEX in MARRIAGE

Sola & Nike Ajayi

ISBN - 978-978-780-481-0

Published by:
Heart2World Publishing
Ago Palace Way. Lagos
w. heart2worldpublishing.org
t. 09056183960
e. heart2worldpublishing@gmail.com

Unless otherwise stated, scripture quotations are from The Holy Bible: King James Version. Cambridge, 1769. Used by permission. All rights reserved.

For information on distribution, translation or bulk sales, please contact:

Sola Ajayi
Phone:+2348023415303, 08023415645
Email: therealmtribe@gmail.com

Dedication

This book is specially dedicated to the husbands and wives who have chosen to be super heroes when it comes to being intentional about satisfying their spouses sexually according to God's will.

These are men and women who have decided to break the cultural, religious and biological barriers, and have become spiritual in handling their sexual lives through intentionality, awareness, and patience.

You are uncommon husbands and wives.

Acknowledgement

The impact and benefit of this book cannot go unsaid without the inspiration of the Holy Spirit. We are grateful to God for practically teaching us by Himself about this unspoken aspect of marriage in Christendom. It's one aspect of marriage that many married couples shy away from discussing among themselves.

We are immeasurably grateful to Pastors Bisi and Yomi Adewale for encouraging us to write this book. Your push is the miracle we need to positively affect many more couples' sexual experiences.

To our co-labourer in faith and calling, whom God used as a handlifter in this project, Pastor Seyi Igunsabi-Perez, we say thank you for being a great blessing. This wouldn't have been done in such a short time without your great input.

Our appreciation, as always, goes to our pastors, ministry

mentors, and spiritual parents who saw the seed of ministry in us and fanned it to flame. Thank you, Pastors Ayo and Adeola Ajisola, for your consistent prayers, support, and counsel over the years.

Pastor J.T. Kalejaiye, you are one in a million father! We can't thank you enough for the gift of access, sir. Your constant encouragement and words have helped us remain focused on the assignment.

To our Regional Pastor in RCCG Region 31, Pastor and Pastor Mrs. Joseph and Felicia Adeyokunnu, thank you, daddy and mummy, for your prayers, love, and support always. What an honour and privilege to have encountered you.

Immense thanks to Pastors Seun and Uchenna Aderibigbe, our Provincial Pastors for their support of our ministry. We are grateful for your support and kind understanding, especially in ensuring we show up whenever we are invited to minister in other places.

Our appreciation can't be complete without mentioning Pastors Yemi and Folake Lebi. Working directly with you for a few years taught us efficiency and excellence. Thank you for your encouragement and prayers.

We appreciate Pastors Peter and Victoria Adedeji for

giving us their support and encouragement. Your belief in our ministry goes a long way.

To the one who is immortal, eternal and the King of kings. Thank you for the grace and strength to write instructively on this title.

Every time God gives a gift to His children, the devil will want to use the gift against them, turning it into a place of battle and difficulties. If there is any place where this is true, it is about sex in marriage.

God created sex to be enjoyable, loving, and a thing to bring couples together and strengthen their union. If there is any area in which couples fight more, it is sex in marriage, second only to money and financial issues. Sex in marriage is holy, it is righteous, it is something to enjoy regularly, and it should not be a bone of contention in marriage.

Couples should know what it is, how to do it regularly, and how to get the most out of it. Like any other area of life, if you want to enjoy it to the maximum and be blessed by it, you must know how to do it, enjoy it, and use it to build up your marriage.

That is why this book, The ABC of Intentional Sex in Marriage, is coming at the right time to help couples build their marriages and teach them how to get the most from the gift of God called SEX .

This book reflects the mind of God about sex in marriage, and it is also science based.

Your spouse wants you to be a great bedroom performer; he or she wants you to be extraordinary in the bedroom, creative, tantalising, and tasty. Make your bedroom what it is supposed to be. Sex in marriage is one thing that must be right if marriage is to be wonderful.

If you want the best in your bedroom, let your thinking be right about sex in marriage. Sex is not evil; it is not ungodly if it is done within the four walls of marriage. It is the foundation of bliss at home.

In this new book, you will learn how to think rightly about sex in marriage.

I recommend this book to all married couples that want to enjoy the best of all sex in their marriages and enjoy tantalising and bed-shaking bedroom performances in their home.

Bisi Adewale

Author of Fight for That Marriage.

Content

INTRODUCTION

Shhhh, please put off the light, his wife requested. As he made his approach to come back to bed to meet her, she noticed the window was opened. Her mood gave Paul an idea of what could be the issue again, so he got up to shut the window.

"I am tired of how Stella reacts whenever we want to make love," Paul retorted.

There are quite a number of couples whose sex lives are stereotyped, uninteresting, and lack improvement. This aspect of our marital life is one we seldom talk about, yet it is germane to the health of our marriage.

Culture and religion have made many couples shy away from discussing their sexual orientation, passions and priorities in order to give each other memorable sexual satisfaction. Sexual pleasure is God's desire for all married couples.

A major anomaly is the fact that the devil has made fornication and adultery an "attractive distraction" to our faith walk and work, while sex in marriage, which ought to be the only atmosphere for having sexual satisfaction, has been downplayed!

We are not nurtured as people to improve our sexual lives, discuss it, and ask if our partner is enjoying it. This is an "attractive" - distraction from the enemy.

This book is written to address the many discussions and tutorials around sex that couples find difficult or "sinful" to discuss and express.

God desires that the sexual altar of His children should be alive and burning as much as their spiritual altar because your sexual relationship is a form of worship to Him.

Proverbs 5:15-19
Drink water from your own cistern, running water from your own well.
Should your springs overflow in the streets, your streams of water in the public squares?
Let them be yours alone, never to be shared with strangers.
May your fountain be blessed, and may you rejoice in the wife of your youth.
A loving doe, a graceful deer may her breasts satisfy you always, may you ever be intoxicated with her love.

We encourage you to read this together as a couple so that your sexual life will be ignited.

We honour you.
Sola & Nike Ajayi

CHAPTER ONE

WHAT SEX IS AND IS NOT IN MARRIAGE

01

What is Sex?

What does the term "sex" mean to you? It's a question that carries a weighty significance, especially for those who are married or planning to be. Depending on our experiences, whether they stem from our formative years, our marital journey, or even the times before marriage, the concept of sex can elicit a range of emotions and interpretations.

Sex, as an integral aspect of marriage, isn't as baffling as some might think. In fact, it's a beautiful and purposeful facet of married life that can bring immense joy when approached with the right mindset. It's the most intimate way a couple can connect with each other, transcending physical boundaries and diving deep into their emotional and spiritual cores.

Sex starts in the mind before it becomes a physical act. It's an exchange of emotions and energies that eventually manifests in the physical realm. And don't forget the spiritual dimension—when two people come together in this profoundly intimate manner, they unite not only their bodies but also their spirits and souls. This fusion is something sacred and powerful.

Sex isn't just about the physical mechanics; it's about the essence of your masculinity or femininity. It's a rejuvenating experience that revitalises both your body and soul. There's a sense of safety attached to it—after all, you're sharing something deeply personal with another person, a vulnerability that's reserved for someone you trust. And that's where the obligation comes in. Each partner owes it to the other to treat this act with respect and decency, as a sacred pact of love. It's a far cry from the explicit and sensationalised portrayals we often encounter in the media.

Consider sexual intercourse as a form of intimate worship, a spiritual merging of two individuals. It's an act that goes beyond the physical, symbolising the connection of hearts and souls. To truly cultivate a strong sexual bond, a couple must be willing to be vulnerable with each other—honesty and openness are key. In a way, your understanding of what sex truly means serves as the compass guiding your approach to this integral component of your marital union. It sets the tone for your anticipation and readiness for such encounters.

Yet, regrettably, a significant number of couples approach sex with a nonchalant attitude and a lack of understanding. This attitude often leads to dullness and dissatisfaction in their sexual lives. As counsellors, we've witnessed people misuse sex due to a lack of comprehension about its purpose.

Interestingly, the devil recognizes the potent power and significance of sexual intimacy between humans. It's a force as profound as worship itself. Perhaps that's why there's an insidious push to divert people towards extramarital sex, undermining the sanctity of sex within marriage. It's no wonder that instances of fornication and adultery are rampant.

It's puzzling to see how the unmarried eagerly anticipate sex with their non-marital partners, while many married couples struggle to maintain the same level of enthusiasm. As soon as singles transition to married life, we've observed a drop in their eagerness for a fulfilling sexual relationship. Excuses start piling up, ranging from stress to pregnancy. The truth is, when the connection isn't rooted in deep love and intimacy, sex can lose its lustre. It's vital to address this disconnect.

The divine Creator of sex within marriage designed it to be a beautiful, bonding experience. However, ignorance has allowed the enemy to sow confusion and distortion. Have you ever pondered why this is the case? It often boils down to a lack of awareness regarding the purpose of sex in marriage and an inadequate understanding of your partner's sexual inclinations.

This piece, co-authored by my husband and myself, aims to lend a helping hand to couples grappling with challenges in their sexual intimacy. We believe that shedding light on the true essence and significance of sex in marriage can contribute to a more fulfilling, harmonious, and joyous union.

Sex is a responsibility for the married.

It is a profound commitment that goes beyond just physical pleasure. This understanding is especially crucial for young people who might not yet be equipped to handle the complexities that come with such responsibilities. Abstaining from sex before marriage isn't about denying desires but rather about acknowledging the maturity and preparedness required to navigate the intricacies of a marital relationship. By doing so, young people are giving themselves the time and space to grow, both individually and emotionally, before embarking on the journey of marriage and all it entails.

That is why young people who are not ready to take on responsibilities must abstain from sex before marriage. Sex was created for marriage; marriage was not made for sex, so marriage is more than just enjoying sex.

Sexuality is undoubtedly an integral aspect of human nature, and it finds its rightful place within the institution of marriage. However, it's important to recognize that the purpose of marriage goes far beyond just the gratification of sexual desires. Marriage is a union of two individuals who commit to sharing their lives in the fullest sense, through companionship, support, and mutual growth. Thus, entering into a marital bond is a decision that carries not only the expectation of physical intimacy but also a profound promise to be there for each other in times of joy, sorrow, and all the moments in between.

Hence, when couples decide to marry and, in turn, engage

in sexual intimacy, they embrace the responsibility that comes with it. Moreover, it entails being prepared to handle the potential outcomes of their physical intimacy, including the possibility of childbirth. In essence, the act of getting married and engaging in sexual relations signifies a commitment to face life's uncertainties with a shared strength, forging a bond that encompasses both the joys and obligations that come with marriage.

Sex is an obligation.

One of the underlying truths about sex in marriage is that it is an obligation. In other words, it is a duty from the husband to the wife and from the wife to her husband. That is why sex starvation is an aberration to sexual intimacy in marriage. The Word of God even cautioned couples against it.

Sex is kind of like an important promise in a marriage – an obligation that both partners have to each other. It's like a special duty that husbands and wives share. Imagine it as a bridge that connects them emotionally, spiritually, and of course, physically too. This connection is like a symbol of their journey together.

So, in the Bible, there's this part in 1 Corinthians 7:3-5 that talks about sex as an obligation. It reads:

1 Corinthians 7:3-5
"Let the husband render to his wife the affection DUE her, and likewise also the wife to her husband.
The wife does not have authority over her own body, but the husband does. And likewise, the husband does not have authority over his own body, but the wife does.
Do not deprive one another except with consent for a time, that you may give yourselves to fasting and prayer; and come together again so that Satan does not tempt you because of your lack of self-control."

It says that husbands should give their wives the affection they owe them, and wives should do the same for their husbands. It's like saying, "Hey, you have a responsibility to make sure your partner's needs are met." The word 'DUE' here is a bit like a spotlight – it shows that this is something you're supposed to do, not just when you're in the mood, but as part of being a partner.

But you know, life gets busy and sometimes couples forget about this obligation. They might think it's not a big deal to skip this part of their relationship. But here's the thing – when this obligation is ignored, it can create distance between partners. The connection they share might start to weaken, and that's not good for the relationship.

Marriage is like a special place where promises live. By keeping up with the obligation of sex, partners are actually showing how much they care for each other. It's not just a routine thing; it's a way of saying, *"I'm committed to you, no matter what."* This isn't about being robotic – it's about making sure your relationship is strong and happy. Even when life gets crazy, remembering this obligation can actually make your bond even stronger.

In today's world, there are so many things vying for our attention. But taking a moment to think about the importance of intimacy in a marriage can really make a difference. Looking at sex as an obligation doesn't make it less exciting or loving; it's just a reminder that you're there for each other in a special way.

When you understand this as a couple, you are not just helping yourself, you are setting an example for everyone around you. Because strong and happy relationships make the whole world a better place.

Sex is a covenant.

Think about sex as a covenant, a deep-rooted promise that goes beyond just physical intimacy. When two people get married, it's like they're exchanging vows not just through words, but through their bodies as well. It's a connection that runs deeper than we often realise. This covenant of intimacy demands the utmost dedication from both partners involved. Unfortunately, not all couples treat it with the seriousness it deserves.

Imagine this covenant like a sacred agreement, a pact that binds two people together in a unique and profound way. But here's the thing – many couples today don't fully grasp the weight of this commitment. Over time, we've witnessed a trend where people, from one generation to the next, break this special bond by engaging in sexual relationships outside of their marriage. The consequences of this breach are far-reaching, impacting marriages and individuals more than they could ever have anticipated.

The Bible, in Genesis 2:24, touches upon this concept beautifully: *"Therefore a man shall leave his father and mother and be joined to his wife, and they shall become one flesh."* This "one flesh" phrase isn't just about physical closeness; it's about merging two lives into a single partnership. Picture it as weaving two distinct threads into a single, unbreakable fabric. In light of this, sex isn't something to be taken lightly, a mere source of pleasure or a casual pastime within marriage.

Rather, it's an integral part of nurturing and reinforcing

the covenant that unites a husband and wife. Just like any commitment, it requires effort, respect, and a deep understanding of the promises made. When we engage in intimate moments with our spouse, we're not just sharing physical pleasure; we're reaffirming the sacred connection that makes our bond unique. It's a shared journey of love, trust, and mutual respect that shapes the very foundation of a marriage.

So, let's think about sex as more than just a physical act. Let's recognize it as a covenant, a sacred promise that deserves our highest respect and commitment. By honouring this covenant, we not only strengthen our marriages but also set an example for future generations – a legacy of profound love and unwavering dedication.

Sex is for pleasure.

Sex isn't just about making babies or ticking off a box on your marital checklist. It's about pleasure—yours and your partner's. But here's the thing: a lot of couples end up missing out on this awesome part of their relationship. They get stuck in this mindset where sex feels like a duty rather than something enjoyable. And you know what? That's not how it's supposed to be!

Imagine if you viewed sex as something exciting,

something that brings pleasure to both you and your partner. That's the perspective we're aiming for here. We're talking about turning things around so that sex becomes something you both look forward to, not just something you feel like you have to do. Who wants boring and routine when it comes to intimacy?

Did you know that our bodies are wired for pleasure? Yep, it's true. We've got all these special parts and chemicals in our bodies that basically shout, "Hey, let's have a good time!" And guess what? Even Scriptural verses like Genesis 26:8 and Proverbs 5:15-19 talk about the importance of finding joy and satisfaction in intimate relationships.

"The men particularly must understand that sex is not just for procreation but for pleasure, thereby taking responsibility to help their wives climax (in pleasure) whenever she wants to. Among other things, a man must understand what turns his wife on and lead her to the pinnacle of pleasure during sex. Understanding the basics of female anatomy can totally help with that.

But it's not just about one person doing all the work. This is a team effort, a partnership. You and your significant other have the chance to explore and figure out what makes both of you tick. Think about it like this: when you enjoy something, you want to do it more, right? It's the same with sex. When you're both having a great time, you'll naturally want to do it more often.

There are skills you can learn that can turn the pressure of having sex into a whole lot of pleasure. It's about honing in on what gets you both excited and embracing the passion that comes with it. Imagine transforming that "I have to do this" mindset into a "I can't wait to do this" feeling. That's the shift we're aiming for.

Sex is not a chore or a duty—it's a beautiful journey of pleasure and connection. It's about exploring, learning, and growing together in ways that make both of you smile. Turn up the passion, discover what makes you both feel fantastic, and enjoy the amazing adventure of intimacy that's waiting for you.

Sex versus Lovemaking

When it comes to matters of the heart and the bedroom, it's not just about the act itself; it's about the profound connection you create with your partner. It's about transforming a physical encounter into an unforgettable journey of pleasure and emotion. We're talking about the distinction between sex and lovemaking—an often-overlooked difference that has the power to reshape the way we approach intimacy.

Consider these fundamental questions: wWat do you seek in your intimate moments with your partner? Is it merely a fleeting physical release, a temporary thrill? Or do you yearn for something deeper, a connection that goes beyond the physical, into the realm of passionate love and emotional bonding? It's a crucial question, because the path you choose can define the entire landscape of your relationship.

Sex, in its simplest form, is a basic biological act. Even animals engage in it for reproduction. But lovemaking—oh, that's an art. It's a complex expression of love that transcends words. It's the desire to communicate your affection for your partner on a level that goes beyond verbal communication. It's the space where you can pour out all your positive feelings and thoughts, whether through those soft murmurs during the act or in the quiet moments of connection before or after. Lovemaking is a holistic experience, a tapestry woven with threads of physical satisfaction and emotional resonance.

Let's be clear, for us humans, sexual intimacy goes way beyond mere coitus or physical penetration. It's a dance of hearts and minds, a symphony of bodies and souls. To truly understand the difference between sex and lovemaking, let's categorise them as "The Highs of Sex" and "The Depths of Making Love."

The "Highs of Sex" revolve around stimulation and sensory responses. It's about the intensity and quantity of physical pleasure, a focus primarily on the nerves and the immediate sensations. It's that quick thrill, the fireworks that light up the moment, but often leave you wanting more.

On the other hand, the "Depths of Making Love" beckon partners to delve into their minds, bodies, and souls to reach each other's hearts. It's about going beyond the physical sensations and exploring the emotional and spiritual facets of the act. Making love opens the door to addressing hidden issues and inhibitions that may emerge during this deeply intimate connection. It's a journey that transcends the boundaries of the body, a union that merges two souls into one.

Making love is a celebration of your partner's entirety— mind, body, and soul. It's not just about the physical act, but the emotional symphony that accompanies it. Yet, this level of intimacy requires dedication and patience. It's about navigating the ever-changing tides of emotions and understanding that every day brings a unique array of feelings. It's about using those feelings to guide your actions during lovemaking, creating an experience that's deeply personal and passionately connected.

The beauty of lovemaking lies in its authenticity. It's not about impressing your partner with feats of Olympic prowess; it's about baring your soul to them in the most genuine way. When you're in sync with each other, when you truly know each other's desires and preferences, lovemaking becomes a dance of souls—an artistry of emotions and connection.

And here's a little secret: intuition is your greatest ally. Let your instincts guide you during lovemaking, and you'll find yourself tapping into a wellspring of creativity you never knew existed. No more worrying about repetition or the next move. Instead, you'll be in sync, moving in harmony, each touch and caress an authentic expression of your love and desire.

Sex without love is not lovemaking. It's a reality that many couples face, sometimes unknowingly. It's a hollow experience that lacks the depth of connection and emotion that comes with lovemaking. Whether you've been together for years or decades, cultivating an emotional bond through lovemaking transforms the act into a purposeful communion. It's a chance to truly be yourself with your partner, to express your desires and emotions freely.

It's very easy and ordinary to just have sex, but to know how to connect with a partner, especially a woman, on a deeper level and win over the heart, mind and soul, takes a little bit of commitment and patience.

Your feelings and thoughts of her will be different every day, and using those feelings to determine what you do during lovemaking will have an added benefit. Sex is biomechanical and instinctive; we all know how to do it. Love making is slow, sensual, and not goal oriented which allows us to experience the metaphysical being of oneness; this type of love making is truly an art in itself. And it is usually done with patience and process for it to yield a priceless memory.

And here's a truth we can learn from unlikely places: consider the interaction between a prostitute and a client. It's a purely mechanical transaction, devoid of emotional resonance. The memories from such encounters often fade quickly. Now compare that to lovemaking—it's an investment in your relationship, a journey that leads to cherished memories that bond you even closer.

For those striving to become great lovemakers, there's a journey of exploration ahead. It's a lifelong pursuit of understanding, especially when it comes to the intricacies of female sexual anatomy. Great lovemakers have an innate awareness of the inner workings of their own bodies as well as those of their partners. They sync with their lover's movements, intuitively creating an experience that transcends the physical realm.

And wives, take heed: there's a distinction between sex and making love. Your influence, character, and position in your husband's life are powerful tools. Understanding and embracing these aspects can empower you to become a truly winning wife, creating a connection that goes beyond the superficial.

In the end, the distinction between sex and lovemaking is not just a matter of semantics—it's a choice. It's a choice to elevate your intimacy, to dive into the depths of emotional connection and passion. It's a choice to cherish each other, to evolve together as passionate lovers and partners.

So, as you embark on this journey of connection, remember that lovemaking is an art—an art that paints memories, deepens bonds, and nurtures the flame of passion in the heart of your relationship.

SEX and the Mind

02

"Now, getting down to the questions you asked in your letter to me. First, is it a good thing to have sexual relations? Certainly, but only within a certain context. It's good for a man to have a wife and for a woman to have a husband. SEXUAL DRIVES ARE STRONG, BUT MARRIAGE IS STRONG ENOUGH TO CONTAIN THEM AND PROVIDE FOR A BALANCED AND FULFILLING SEXUAL LIFE IN A WORLD OF SEXUAL DISORDER."- 1 Corinthians. 7:1-2 (Message Bible)

The scriptures above make it clear that it is God's will for us to have a great, balanced, and fulfilling sexual life. In our generation, like it was with the old, there is so much sexual disorder, perversion, and abnormality that one wonders if sex could still be had in sane, righteous and enjoyable ways in times like this.

A game-changer in the world of intimacy is the mind. When it comes to sex, it's not just about the physical actions—it all starts and ends in the mind. Sounds a bit surprising, right? But trust me, your mind is like the superhero behind the scenes, working hand in hand with those powerful hormones to set the stage for some amazing experiences.

Sex isn't this isolated event that happens between the sheets. It actually kicks off way before and keeps echoing in your mind even after. Those hormones, they're like the orchestra, and your mind is the conductor. The magic of marital intimacy lies in how well you nurture your mind to embrace and welcome a satisfying sex life within the realm of marriage.

Let's take lessons from 2 Peter 1:3 in the Bible:
His divine power has given us everything required for life and godliness through the knowledge of Him who called us by His own glory and goodness.

It talks about God's divine power giving us everything we need for life and godliness. And guess what? God's got marriage covered too. He's like the ultimate matchmaker, and He's given us the tools to enjoy our sexual lives if we're willing to embrace them.

Ever wondered why there's a whole book in the Bible dedicated to romance - the Song of Solomon? That's God giving a nod to the importance of our emotional and sexual well-being. He's not shy about talking about this stuff, so we shouldn't be either.

Sex within the bounds of marriage isn't just a physical act—it's also a sacred bond, a form of worship between you and your partner, and yeah, even between you and the Big Guy up there. That's why treating your sexual intimacy with respect and understanding matters. It's not something to be taken lightly. When your spiritual and sexual connections are on point, you've got this unbeatable team dynamic going on.

But, here's the thing: you've got to be the master of your own mind. It's like honing a skill. You need the right mindset to approach sex in marriage, to make it a true bonding experience, and to find maximum pleasure in it. It's all about seeing the bigger picture and understanding the role of sex in the beautiful journey of marriage.

Here are some practical steps that can help you supercharge your mindset and become a pro at using sex as a tool not just for a successful marriage but also for your own satisfaction and fulfilment.

YOUR PERSONAL HYGIENE

"And the roof of your mouth is like good wine flowing down smoothly for my loved one, moving gently over my lips and my teeth." S.O.S 7:9

Body or mouth odour is something that's often tough to admit. It's pretty common for people to not want to think they have it. But here's the thing, just because you're used to it and it doesn't bother you, doesn't mean your partner feels the same way. Believe it or not, this can actually mess with your intimate moments.

No one likes an unpleasant smell. So, it's a good idea to make sure you're fresh and clean, especially in those important areas. A little grooming can go a long way too. A clean shave can make a difference. And hey, don't forget about your teeth. Visiting the dentist for a bit of cleaning and polishing can do wonders. Plus, don't just brush your teeth—brush your tongue too. If you're dealing with bad breath, there's no shame in seeking help to fix it.

It might sound simple, but these little things can have a big impact. Your partner will definitely appreciate the effort, and it can actually make a real difference in how close you feel during those intimate times. So, embrace the power of good hygiene and let it add a new level of connection to your relationship.

SELF-CONFIDENCE AND APPRECIATION OF YOUR BODY

"I am a wall, and my breasts are like towers; then I was in his eyes as one to whom a good chance had come." S.O.S 8:10.

Don't let your shyness or insecurities mess up a good thing. Believe in yourself and what you've got, because confidence is a magnet. You have to embrace your own awesomeness. If you start thinking your body is just a tool to check off a to-do list, well, that's not the path to a strong, intimate connection with your partner.

Rock that self-assured attitude and appreciate every bit of yourself that makes you unique. God made you just the way you are for a reason, and that includes all those body parts that play a role in the wonderful dance of intimacy. When you own your confidence, you are not just feeling good about yourself, you are also turning up the heat in the bedroom. Your partner will pick up on that vibe, and trust me, they will be loving it.

If you're treating your body like it's just a checklist item for marital duties, you're missing out on the deeper magic of intimacy. Sex is not just about obligation—it is about connection, passion, and embracing each other's whole selves. When you're not comfortable with your own body, it's like a roadblock to the amazing intimacy you could be experiencing.

Think about it this way: confidence is like a secret ingredient that makes everything better. It is the spice that brings out the flavour in your relationship. You've got to be your own biggest fan, celebrating the unique package that you are. And when you do that, you're setting the stage for a vibrant, exciting, and meaningful sex life with your partner.

Don't let shyness or doubts mess with your mojo. Own your confidence, because it's seriously irresistible. Appreciate yourself, inside and out, and don't fall into the trap of thinking you are just ticking boxes. Sex is about more than that—it is a symphony of emotions, sensations, and connection. So, step into your confidence, and get ready to take your intimacy to a whole new level. You've got this!

JERK UP YOUR SEX DRIVE

"As a loving hind and a gentle doe, let her breast ever satisfy you; let your passion at all times be moved by her love."
Prov. 5:19

Dealing with a low sex drive is definitely a thing, and it can seriously mess with how things go down in the bedroom. Before you can rock at this whole sex thing, you've got to get yourself pumped up about it. That means actually wanting to have some fun between the sheets. But here is the sweet part—once you are all excited and ready to roll, your partner gets in on the action too, and it's way better than just going through the motions.

Think about it like this: when you're genuinely up for some bedroom action, it's not just a regular ol' routine. It becomes this awesome memory you and your partner share. It is like this super cool event you both eagerly look forward to. Those moments that stick with you, making you smile when you think about them later.

The real secret sauce is finding that motivation. It is like unlocking a whole new level of awesome in your relationship. When you are both on the same page, wanting to make these memories together, things get seriously exciting. It is not about just doing it because you have to—it is about doing it because you really, truly want to.

It's not just about being good at the *physical* stuff. It is about the emotional connection, the thrill of sharing something special with your partner. So, if you are feeling that low drive, don't sweat it. Focus on what gets you excited, what makes you look forward to those intimate moments. Because when you're both motivated and ready to enjoy, that is when the magic really happens.

VARIETY AND FLEXIBILITY

"Come, my beloved, Let us go forth to the field; Let us lodge in the villages. Let us get up early to the vineyards; Let us see if the vine has budded, Whether the grape blossoms are open, And the pomegranates are in bloom. There I will give you my love." Song of Songs 7:11-12.

It is absolutely fine to not always be in the mood for romance round the clock. I mean, who wouldn't want to just kick back and relax after a tiring day at work? While it's okay to have those moments, it's not a great idea to let it become a regular thing. It's like, sure, take a breather, but don't make it a routine.

Every now and then, surprise your partner with

something fresh and exciting. You know how it goes – after a while, the same old routine can get a bit stale. Your partner might even start predicting your moves like a mind reader! And trust me, you don't want your bedroom turning into a boredom zone. So, mix things up a bit! Try out new ideas, be a little adventurous – it could add a spark you never knew was missing.

Do not forget about boundaries. It's crucial to keep things within a safe zone. You've got your spiritual life as a child of God to consider, and of course, your physical well-being too. We are bombarded with all sorts of ideas about what's right and what's not when it comes to sex. It's pretty important stuff because in this age of information, there's this trend of pushing the limits in ways that might not be so godly. It's become quite a hot topic, actually.

1 Corinthians 6:12

"Glorify God in Body and Spirit
All things are lawful for me, but all things are not helpful. All things are lawful for me, but I will not be brought under the power of any."

Romans 1:26-28

"For this reason God gave them up to vile passions. For even their women exchanged the natural use for what is against

nature.

Likewise also the men, leaving the natural use of the woman, burned in their lust for one another, men with men committing what is shameful, and receiving in themselves the penalty of their error which was due.

And even as they did not like to retain God in their knowledge, God gave them over to a debased mind, to do those things which are not fitting;"

HONEST AND LOVING COMMUNICATION

It's not uncommon for couples to hit a bit of a boredom slump in their sex lives. It's like they're in a maze without the map, stumbling around because they haven't quite figured out what gets their partner all fired up. And you know what? A big part of this confusion stems from a lack of communication.

Picture this: you're trying to put together a jigsaw puzzle, but you're missing some key pieces. Those missing pieces are like the things you and your partner haven't talked about when it comes to your sexual desires and preferences. It's like expecting your partner to read your mind, when in reality, they can't even find the first piece of that puzzle. This lack of communication doesn't just stay out of the bedroom—it sneaks its way right in.

Communication during those intimate moments is like having a secret map to that puzzle. It's like whispering the secrets of your desires and needs to each other, unlocking a whole new level of connection. Think about it this way: you and your partner are explorers, and your bodies are the uncharted territory. Talking and listening to each other during sex is like charting new territories together, discovering what makes each other tick.

Imagine you're trying to make a really special meal for your partner. You wouldn't just guess what ingredients they like, right? You'd ask them, figure out what spices make their taste buds dance. Well, guess what? The same principle applies to sex. Instead of assuming your partner knows every little detail about your sexuality, have a chat about it. Ask questions, share your thoughts, and let them do the same. It's like unveiling a treasure map and following it together to find the hidden gems of pleasure.

When you communicate lovingly during those intimate moments, something magical happens. It's like the entire experience gains a sense of purpose. You're not just going through the motions; you're actively seeking to bring pleasure and happiness to each other. It's like you're partners in this grand adventure of pleasure, each making sure the other is having an amazing time.

But there's more to it. When you open up and talk with your partner, you're not just enriching your physical connection. You're also boosting your emotional bond. It's like a two-for-one deal! By being open, vulnerable, and lovingly expressive, you're building trust and intimacy that extend far beyond the bedroom walls.

If you want to keep the spark alive, if you want to banish that boredom and discover new heights of pleasure, start by having those conversations.

Share your desires, ask about theirs, and together, you'll embark on a journey of connection and satisfaction that will make your relationship stronger than ever before. Communication isn't just talking—it's igniting the flame of desire and setting your passion on a path of purpose.

CHAPTER THREE

The ABC of SEX in Marriage

03

"Sex will often go wrong or be unsatisfactory for both the man and the woman when these sex hormones are not well secreted during coitus."

When it comes down to it, sex and lovemaking have the potential to be amazing experiences for all couples. Seriously, it's like this hidden treasure that's right there, waiting to be discovered. But here's the thing: understanding the ins and outs of sex is key. It's like having a secret map to unlock a world of pleasure and connection. You might wonder why on earth God made such a big deal about sex within marriage? Well, turns out, there are some pretty good reasons behind it.

A lot of couples end up stumbling when it comes to their sex lives. It's like they missed the memo on how awesome it could be. And you know what's the saddest part? It's often because they're not giving sex the respect it deserves in their marriage. You see, just like anything in life, when you don't treat it right, things can go south real fast. And that's exactly why so many couples find themselves stuck in this rut of lacklustre intimacy.

Not giving sex the attention it deserves is like planting a beautiful garden and then never bothering to water it. It's no wonder that the spark fizzles out and things become a little dull. But here's the thing that's even more concerning: this casual attitude towards sex isn't just about missing out on some steamy nights. Nope, it's bigger than that. It's causing serious trouble in paradise for so many couples out there.

You've got to realise that when you ignore the purpose behind something, it's like inviting trouble to knock on your door. And that's exactly what's happening in the bedrooms of so many couples. Intimacy becomes this forgotten thing, and suddenly, it's like you're just going through the motions. No wonder things get complicated. It's like trying to drive a car without any fuel—it's not going to get you very far.

Fortunately, the good, the bad, and the awkward are fixable. It's like having a messy room that just needs a bit of organising. We have got some secrets to spill, some insights that can totally transform your sexual intimacy game. We have been counselling couples for fifteen years, hearing about their ups and downs, and let me tell you, there's a pattern that emerges.

We like to call it the ABCs of sex in marriage. It's like this roadmap that can guide you to a whole new level of intimacy.

Appreciate and Accept Each Other's Bodies.

When it comes to building a strong and fulfilling sexual connection with your partner, appreciating and accepting each other's physical forms is essential. Whether your partner is tall or short, curvy or lean, with a skin tone that's light, dark, or somewhere in between—embrace who they are, inside and out. It's all about looking past the external, beyond the surface. Because real love, the kind that matters, goes way beyond appearances. Those physical traits we put so much weight on are bound to change over time, like everything else does. That's just part of being human, and it's something we all share.

One of the things that can chip away at the intimacy in a relationship is this nagging dissatisfaction with how our partner looks. It's like this loop that plays in our heads, focusing on things like body shape or specific body parts. It might sound strange, but you'd be surprised how many couples get caught up in this cycle. Honestly, that's not where you want your head to be when you're trying to connect on an intimate level.

Here's the scoop for couples who are really looking to take their sexual connection to the next level: accept your partner's physical self, quirks and all. Even if they don't match some idealised version you had in your head before you tied the knot. I mean, think about it—do you really want to spend your time stressing over how your partner's body looks when you're about to get close? That's a pretty draining way to approach things.

You have to bring contentment into the picture if you're serious about nurturing a thriving sexual bond. It means finding satisfaction in what you have, where you are, and who you're with. That applies to your marriage and your sexual life too. If you are a believer, you are probably familiar with the idea of finding contentment in every aspect of your life. Well, guess what? That includes your marriage and your intimate moments.

Life can throw us some curveballs. Take a woman who's been through a C-section during childbirth. That kind of experience can lead to changes in her body that she never saw coming, especially in the abdominal area. Or consider a man who starts to develop a bit of a belly after saying "I do." It might not be something his wife initially thought was attractive. And let's not forget about the size and shape of those sexual organs we often obsess over—breasts, penis, thighs, hips, buttocks. They might not fit the "ideal" that we've built up in our minds. But here's the thing: those changes, those differences, they're part of the journey.

It's about making a choice, a conscious decision. Choose to embrace and appreciate your partner beyond the surface. Let them know how much they mean to you, not just in words but in actions. Shower them with kindness, let them feel your love and acceptance because building intimacy, real intimacy, is about connecting on a level that goes beyond the physical. It's about being vulnerable, showing that you're there for each other no matter what and that kind of connection is what makes those intimate moments truly special.

A journey toward a deeper, richer connection with your partner that starts with accepting and cherishing each other's bodies. It's a journey that's rooted in contentment, in seeing beyond the ever-changing surface and embracing the beauty of your shared love story. And remember, the path to intimacy is one that's built on respect, love, and a whole lot of acceptance.

Browse and Be Browseable.

You've probably heard the phrase "browse and be browseable" tossed around, but what exactly does it mean? In simple terms, it's about getting into the groove of foreplay and fully enjoying every moment of it. Foreplay is like the appetiser before the main course—it sets the stage for amazing intimacy between you and your partner. You wouldn't want to skip this step if you're aiming for a satisfying and mind-blowing experience in the bedroom.

Picture this: you and your partner are gearing up for a steamy encounter. But here's the thing, it's not just about diving right in. You need to warm things up, get those engines revving, and set the stage for some serious pleasure. That's where foreplay comes into play. Think of it as a delicate dance of tender touches in those oh-so-sensitive areas that send shivers down your spine. We are talking about those spots that have the power to make your heart race and your toes curl.

Foreplay isn't a one-size-fits-all deal. It's more like a personalised journey of discovery. You have the sandpaper touches and the feather-light caresses. The sandpaper touches? Those are like when things get a bit too heated, and you're rushing towards that grand finale.

It's not necessarily a bad thing, but sometimes taking your time can make the destination even sweeter. On the flip side, we have the feather-like touches. These are gentle, deliberate, and oh-so-calculated. They are like whispers of pleasure that guide your partner's arousal, especially when it comes to those spots that hold the key to ultimate satisfaction.

In fact, Song of Songs 6:2-3 from The Message Bible *Never mind. My lover is already on his way to his garden, to browse among the flowers, touching the colours and forms. I am my lover's and my lover is mine. He caresses the sweet-smelling flowers.*

It talks about browsing among the flowers, touching the colours and forms. But don't let your mind drift to a literal garden. This is all about the gentle and pleasurable touch that enhances the experience. It's about connection, anticipation, and making the journey just as exciting as the destination.

The secret ingredient to mind-blowing foreplay is observation. As you're navigating this sea of sensations, take a moment to observe your partner's reactions. Watch how their body moves, their expressions change, and listen to the sounds they make. It's like reading their body's secret language. This feedback loop is like your compass, guiding you towards the ultimate goal—orgasm for both of you.

When it comes to browsing your partner's body, patience is your best friend. Especially for guys, taking your time and truly understanding what makes your partner tick is a game-changer. It might take a bit longer, but trust me, the reward is totally worth it. And remember, orgasm isn't just a finish line; it's a shared experience that seals the deal on an amazing encounter.

This isn't just about technique—it's about creating an environment where both of you feel desired and cherished. It's about breaking down those barriers that sometimes creep into the bedroom. No one should feel like just an object of pleasure or frustration. If someone's feeling unsatisfied, it's like a leak in the ship of intimacy.

Browsing and being browseable is a journey of connection and exploration. It's about savouring every moment, listening to your partner's cues, and unleashing pleasure in its most exquisite form. And this isn't just a one-time thing; it's a practice that can transform your intimacy into a realm of fulfilment and closeness. Toss aside those unsatisfying notions and embark on a journey of intimate discovery that'll have both you and your partner saying, "Wow, that was amazing."

Come to Canaan

Embarking on the journey of understanding sexual intimacy within the context of a Christian marriage, we find ourselves standing at a pivotal crossroads—a juncture that invites us to explore the concept of "Coming to Canaan." Just as the land of Canaan, as depicted in the Bible, overflows with abundance, symbolising a realm flowing with milk and honey, we shall draw a parallel between this lush land and the zenith of physical and emotional connection that is attainable between Christian couples. In this pursuit, we shall navigate the intricacies of sexual gratification, drawing insights from the profound wisdom of scripture.

As we delve into the heart of this matter, an inquiry emerges: what precisely does it mean to "Come to Canaan" in the realm of marital intimacy? This intriguing notion conjures images of unimpeded exhilaration, akin to the unhampered flow of life-sustaining fluids coursing through the human body. In our quest for deeper understanding, let us embark on a voyage that traverses the terrain of sexual excitement, arousal, and the intricate interplay of hormones that orchestrate the symphony of intimacy.

It is an irrefutable truth that sexual pleasure is a vital

component of the marital bond, one that carries the potential to elevate the human experience to a plane of exquisite ecstasy. Yet, it is not uncommon for couples, particularly wives, to encounter challenges when endeavouring to attain the pinnacle of sexual gratification during intercourse. This challenge can often be attributed to the delicate balance of sex hormones—substances that bear a pivotal role in orchestrating the multifaceted dance of intimacy. The significance of these hormones cannot be overstated; they are the secret behind the harmonious choreography of sexual interactions.

Essentially, these hormones function as nature's lubricants, facilitating the seamless union of sexual organs, particularly the vaginal walls of a woman, during the act of coitus. The presence of adequate lubrication, nurtured through affectionate foreplay, serves as a catalyst for unhindered penetration. The application of tenderness, from gentle caresses to intimate kisses, primes the path for arousal, rendering penetration not only feasible but immensely pleasurable. In essence, the state of proper lubrication paves the way for a mutually fulfilling experience, an intricate dance of pleasure and intimacy.

An intriguing facet of this narrative is the phenomenon of orgasm—a transcendent climax of pleasure that has intrigued human beings across generations. It is noteworthy that, for some women, reaching orgasm is not a solitary pursuit; rather, it is intertwined with the rhythm of flowing penetration, preceded by a harmonious symphony of foreplay orchestrated by their spouses. Herein lies the harmony of desire and response, where mastery of the art of foreplay becomes the key to unlocking the door to shared ecstasy.

Conversely, the absence of these vital hormones can lead to a disheartening experience, often characterised by discomfort and pain for both partners. The importance of these hormones manifests in their capacity to orchestrate not only physical satisfaction but also emotional fulfilment. It is a symphony in which the mind and body harmonise, catalysing a sequence of reactions that culminate in a crescendo of bliss. This holistic alignment is the cornerstone of the intimate experience, rendering it a harmonious fusion of both the physical and the emotional.

However, the journey to Canaan is not devoid of its challenges. There exists an evident disconnect that permeates some marriages—a detachment born from inadequate foreplay that undermines a woman's ability to relish the voyage to Canaan and fully embrace the climax that is rightfully hers. The resonating truth is that few women would decline an invitation to partake in the journey if they were assured that their husbands were invested in their pleasure, akin to traversing the landscape of foreplay to ensure that they, too, are poised to experience the fulfilment that Canaan offers.

In certain instances, the harmonisation of pleasure reaches a crescendo with both partners simultaneously achieving orgasm—a feat that accentuates the bond between them. This synchronous culmination of pleasure is not only a testament to their intimacy but also a reaffirmation of their connection, a tapestry woven from shared vulnerability and trust. It is a poignant reminder that the canvas of a fulfilling sexual life is multifaceted, with threads of desire and fulfilment interweaving to create a masterpiece of marital unity.

The nexus between physical intimacy and spiritual growth is both intriguing and undeniable. A symbiotic relationship exists between the two altars—an intimate one within the bedroom and the spiritual one within the sanctum of faith. As one thrives, so does the other; they are twin flames, each fueling the other's fervour. A harmonious sexual life extends its influence beyond the realm of the bedroom, impacting the couple's spiritual journey and their connection with a higher power. It is a resonating testament to the intricate interplay between the physical and the metaphysical, a reminder that the sacred and the sensual can coexist harmoniously within the sacred covenant of marriage.

Conversely, a discordant sexual life can cast a shadow upon the spiritual altar, diminishing its vibrancy and resonance. Disharmony in the bedroom reverberates through the spiritual realm, distorting the connection between the couple and their faith. In these moments, the absence of physical intimacy serves as a harbinger of emotional distance, an impediment to the couple's willingness to commune in worship and prayer. It is a stark reminder that the intricate fabric of a healthy relationship is woven with threads of affection, trust, and shared vulnerability.

Indeed, sex, as endowed by the Creator, is a divine gift to marriages—a facet that should neither be neglected nor sought outside its rightful place. The narrative painted by the scriptures echoes the profundity of cherishing and nurturing this gift.

The apostle Paul's words in 1 Corinthians 7:3-5 reverberate through the corridors of time, proclaiming the sanctity of mutual satisfaction and affection within the sacred union of marriage. This sacred injunction, epitomised by the biblical dictum "the two shall become one flesh," speaks to a holistic unity—physically, emotionally, and spiritually.

In light of these profound truths, the imperative of embracing the bounty of Canaan within the context of marital intimacy is abundantly clear. Just as the land of

Canaan symbolises a realm overflowing with abundance, so does the realm of physical and emotional connection within marriage offer the promise of abundant gratification and unity. To "come to Canaan" is to embark upon a journey fueled by mutual respect, unabridged communication, and an ardent desire to cherish and nurture the gift of intimacy that has been bestowed upon the union.

In the pursuit of Canaan, couples find themselves standing at the threshold of a shared adventure, armed with the knowledge that a fulfilling sexual life transcends the physical—it is an embodiment of the divine promise that two shall become one.

As they traverse the landscape of pleasure, desire, and unity, they testify to the profound wisdom of scriptural guidance. The notion that a harmonious sexual altar complements the spiritual one stands as a beacon of hope—a testament to the intricate tapestry that is woven when faith and intimacy unite in holy matrimony. Thus, let us heed the call to "Come to Canaan," where love, pleasure, and sacred unity converge in a symphony of human connection—a masterpiece sculpted by the hands of the Divine Creator.

CHAPTER FOUR

SEX: Intended For Pleasure

04

In the first chapter we mentioned four important thoughts that every couple must uphold about sex. These thoughts are capable of aiding wholesome sexuality in a marital union. They are: sex as a responsibility, an obligation, a covenant and pleasure. This chapter is all about one of those thoughts: Sex is for pleasure.

After sitting down with loads of couples over the years and having some serious heart-to-heart conversations, we have figured out that there is a major problem brewing. It is all about sexual satisfaction—or rather, the lack of it. This issue is not just causing little tiffs between partners; it is causing full-on chaos that is tearing marriages apart, sometimes even more than we can wrap our heads around.

So, what's this whole "sexual dissatisfaction" thing we are

talking about? Well, it is when either the guy or the gal is not really feeling the joy and excitement during sex, you know, not getting that happy ending we all expect. It is like there is this emotional cloud hanging over the whole thing because deep down, we all know that sex is supposed to be an amazing experience, a source of pure satisfaction. But sometimes, it is just not happening.

Sex should be a blast for both the husband and the wife. Nobody has a monopoly on the good vibes—it is a two-way street. And when we say "marriage," we mean exactly that. The magic should totally go down between just the two of you, no outsiders invited.

This is where it gets tricky. When it comes to feeling let down in the bedroom, it is often the ladies who are feeling the brunt more than the guys. Now, don't get us wrong, this is not some blame game. It is just that our biology, emotions, and hormones can sometimes gang up against us, leading to this mismatch between expectation and reality.

Some husbands could use a little tutorial in the art of pleasing their wives. It is not that they are intentionally missing the mark; sometimes, they just never got the memo on how to bring their A-game to the bed. This is a bigger issue than you might think, especially in certain cultural and religious setups.

On the flipside, there are those super cool and caring hubbies who are all about making sure their wives are on cloud nine during sexual intercourse. It is like they are on a mission to make sure their partners are just as thrilled as they are. It is a team effort.

Now, here is the twist: both men and women can hit the brakes during intimacy if it is not hitting the spot anymore. Maybe it is feeling a bit monotonous for the guys or just not satisfying for the ladies. So, if you want to keep the spark alive, if you want sex to be an awesome, ongoing adventure, you have to be all in. It is about chasing that pleasure without holding back, without any weird restrictions.

Sex is meant to be a blast, a joyride that both of you should totally enjoy. Sometimes life can get in the way, and things might not always be fireworks and magic. But you have to remember that you are in this together, you are a team, and it is all about creating those moments of pure bliss. So go on, make the most out of it, and remember, pleasure is not something to be shy about—it is a gift you both deserve.

This chapter focuses on sex as an act intended for pleasure

by the Originator of man, marriage and sex. From our counselling sessions with couples over the years, one major thing that is causing grudges between couples these days is sexual dissatisfaction. In fact, it is not just causing conflicts in marriages, it is breaking up marital unions and homes beyond comprehension.

Sexual dissatisfaction occurs when, either the man or woman is unable to enjoy and climax during sex often. This emotional negative attitude comes from the fact that everyone practising sex has a foreknowledge that sex is intended for pleasure, maximum satisfaction. It is one thing to have sex, it is another to derive pleasure and satisfaction from it.

Sex should be satisfying to both husbands and wives. None of them has more right to the highest pleasure it gives than the other. In marriage, not outside of it, sex should be mutually and maximally enjoyed by each couple.

When we talk about sexual dissatisfaction, more often than not, the women are the victims of this marital anomaly than the men. Of course, this is due to the difference in their sexual organs biologically, emotional wiring and hormonal behaviours.

Five Ways To Sexually Please Your Husband As A Wife

1. Be sexually confident.

Imagine stepping into your bedroom, knowing that it is time to share an intimate moment with your spouse. There is absolutely no need for shyness here. If you are married, you have every right to confidently approach your partner when it comes to enjoying the pleasures of the bedroom. Marriage is like a safe haven, a space where you and your life partner, who also happens to be your sex partner, can explore the depths of physical connection.

As a wife, do you desire your husband passionately? Do you initiate sex? Or are you waiting around for him to make the move every single time? It might sound surprising, but some women hold the notion that taking the lead in initiating sex somehow undermines their sense of womanhood. Bust that myth right now. Your right to initiate intimacy is as solid as your husband's, and it is high time we put an end to this misconception.

Intimacy is not a one-way street where your husband is the driver and you are just along for the ride. No way! It is about both of you being active participants, each taking the reins at times. You have the power to use your hands, your mouth, your body—everything—to show your love and desire.

Here's a little secret I will let you in on: I used to think that being a devout Christian wife meant I had to suppress my sexual confidence. It took a while, but I realised that I was far from the truth. Being a faithful wife does not mean you have to leave your sexual savvy at the door. In fact, being a Christian wife and being sexually confident can go hand in hand, and it should.

In the realm of marriage, you are not just a wife—you are also his mistress and the one he desires above all else. It is within the boundaries of marriage that the beauty of sex flourishes without a hint of sin. Anything outside this sacred bond is where lines get crossed and hearts are troubled. But when you step into your marriage bed, you are stepping into a sanctuary where sexual intimacy can be celebrated with all its fervour and joy.

If you are feeling a bit uncertain about how to bolster your sexual confidence, don't worry—there is good news. Learning and growing in this area is absolutely possible. Just like you have learned and grown in other aspects of life, you can do the same here. It is about exploring, communicating with your partner, and discovering what brings both of you pleasure.

Remember, sexual confidence is not about being flashy or bold—it is about embracing your desires, honouring your partner, and cultivating a deeper connection. It is about recognizing that intimacy is an essential part of your relationship, a tapestry woven with threads of emotional, spiritual, and physical connection.

Break free from outdated beliefs. Embrace your role as a confident and empowered partner in the bedroom. It is not just about him initiating or you following—it is about sharing a journey where both of you take turns leading and exploring. And as you do so, you are not just nurturing your marital bond, but you are also fostering a sense of liberation that allows you to fully embrace your identity as a woman, a wife, and a lover.

2. Enjoy your orgasm and his orgasm.

This is something that is often whispered about in hushed tones—the big "O" - Orgasm. It might not be the only thing that matters, but it holds a lot of weight in the world of intimacy. I have always believed that. Now, I know not every woman feels the need to reach that pinnacle every single time they get intimate, and that is totally okay. But I cannot help raising an eyebrow when I hear a wife say she couldn't care less about climaxing. Seriously?

Imagine this: you are in a moment of deep spiritual connection, maybe during worship, and you feel this overwhelming rush that just lifts you up. Well, think of an orgasm like that. It is a rush of sensations that can transport you to another realm. That is why I like to think of satisfying and pleasurable sex as a form of worship. You are honouring each other's bodies, and in a way, your shared activity becomes an offering to the divine. Connecting your physical and spiritual selves can be incredibly powerful.

A sexual encounter without that pleasure can feel a bit like a ship lost at sea—more warship than worship. God had this genius idea of gifting us with orgasmic pleasure for marriage. It is a natural high, if you will. If it is part of God's design, why don't we pursue it with the same fervour we would chase after any blessing from the Creator? When you, as a wife, experience that rush of pleasure, it is not just about you—it's like a resounding "Yes" to your husband. Most husbands feel like superheroes when they know they've brought their wives to that place of ecstasy.

When you climax, you are soaking in satisfaction, and he is wearing that smile of accomplishment because it is not as easy for him as it is for you. And when he reaches that peak too, it is your turn to pat yourself on the back for a job well done. It is like a synchronised dance of pleasure, and you are both the stars of the show.

Orgasms are not just great for your relationship; they are pretty awesome for your health too. It is like a natural stress-buster that can also slow down the clock on ageing. And emotionally, there is a whole cocktail of happiness hormones released—endorphins, dopamine, and oxytocin, to name a few. When you have a healthy sexual life, you can actually radiate that happiness from within.

Picture this: a woman who is truly in sync with her sexual self, glowing with a natural confidence. It is not just about the physical—it is about the emotional and mental well-being too. It is like a harmonious symphony where pleasure resonates through every aspect of your being.

In the grand tapestry of marriage, sexual intimacy is a vital thread. And within that tapestry, orgasm is not just a detail; it is a powerful stroke of colour that adds depth and vibrancy. It is a shared experience that enriches your connection on levels beyond the physical. It is a testament to the beauty of the human body, the intricate design of pleasure, and the divine plan that brought two souls together.

Embrace the journey of pleasure. Allow yourself to

explore the depths of connection that orgasm can offer. Cherish the sensations, the intimacy, and the profound unity that you create. In the realm of relationships, let your love be a masterpiece painted with the hues of pleasure and fulfilment. Your bodies are designed for it, your spirits yearn for it, and your partnership thrives on it.

3. Bring God into the bedroom/sex room.

This is something that might make a lot of people a tad uncomfortable, but it is time to clear the air: sex in the context of Christian marriage. There is this lingering notion that even within the sacred bonds of matrimony, sex is somehow tainted, maybe even a little dirty. Change that belief. It is time to bring some heavenly perspective into your bedroom.

Dear Christian wife, there is a hitch in the game plan if you're letting inhibitions take the wheel in your sexual relationship with your husband. You know what Proverbs 5:18-19 has to say? It's straightforward:

"May your fountain be blessed, and may you rejoice in the wife of your youth. A loving doe, a graceful deer—may her breasts satisfy you always, may you ever be captivated by her love."

The Bible drops some major hints here: it talks about a

"fountain" (which is a discreet way of saying "the male organ"), a wife, breasts, satisfaction, captivation, and love. And none of these words should be linked to inhibition. Instead, they are practically shouting about the joy of marital intimacy.

Don't let this just be words on a page; this is about embracing a divine invitation. Think about it—when you embrace your husband sexually, you are not only saying "Yes" to intimacy, you're saying "Yes" to the Lord. God's presence is not something distant; He is right there with you, even in the bedroom. He is the author of the Book that talks about satisfying your husband, igniting passion, and celebrating the incredible bond you share as husband and wife.

If you are feeling a little shy or hesitant about fully embracing the beauty of sexual intimacy within marriage, you might want to ask yourself if your heart is aligned with God's perspective. The enemy of connection loves to mess with your mind, to quench the fire that is meant to blaze within your relationship. Don't let that happen. Seek out what God has to say about this beautiful gift that is meant for you and your spouse.

When you decide to engage with your husband on a deeper level, you're not just ticking off a box; you're inviting God into that moment. It is like saying, "Hey, we're here, we're connected, and we're celebrating this gift together." God wants you to find joy in each other, to explore the amazing paths of pleasure, and to treasure the intimacy that is a cornerstone of your marriage.

The next time you step into your bedroom, remember that you are not alone. You are sharing that space with the Creator of love and intimacy. Don't hold back; let God's light illuminate your moments of passion and connection. It is time to cast aside those inhibitions and embrace the divine gift of marital intimacy with open hearts, open minds, and a deep understanding of the profound love that brought you together in the first place.

4. Be sexually playful with your clothes on.

This is not about teasing and leaving things hanging; it is about igniting that flame and keeping it alive. Have you ever noticed that sometimes couples forget to turn each other on? Well, good news: marriage gives you a licence to keep that passion alive.

If the idea of being sexually playful seems a bit out of your comfort zone, don't worry – you're not alone. Stepping out of that cosy bubble can lead to some seriously exciting moments.

Here are five ways to be playful with your partner while keeping your clothes on.

1. The gentle bum slap: Picture this: you are walking together or just passing each other by, and you give a little tap on your partner's behind. It is like a playful secret code that only the two of you understand. Of course, it is important to make sure it's just the two of you around – we wouldn't want any awkward moments!

2. Earlobes talks: You know those times when you are watching a movie or having a cosy chat. Start gently playing with each other's earlobes. It might sound simple, but those soft, sweet touches can send shivers down your spine and remind you of how much you enjoy each other's company.

Ever thought of a foot massage as a magical trick? It might not sound explicitly sexual, but trust us, it works wonders. Imagine having a serious conversation while your partner gives you a relaxing foot massage. It is like saying, "I'm here for you, body and soul." It's the kind of connection that builds intimacy even when your clothes are fully on.

3. Adjusting clothing: Imagine you're helping each other with buttons or zippers. Instead of making it routine, turn it into a tantalising game. Look deeply into each other's eyes while you help each other out. It is a moment where the mundane becomes extraordinary.

4. *The back cuddle and neck kiss combo:* Think about those moments when you are getting dressed or just putting on your clothes. Approach your partner from behind, wrap your arms around them, and leave a sweet kiss on the back of their neck. It is like a loving surprise that shows you are still deeply connected, even in the midst of daily routines.

Remember, the key here is playfulness – it is all about having fun and adding a dash of excitement to your relationship. These are small, simple acts that have the power to reignite that flame you might have thought was dimming. So, the next time you're spending time with your partner, give one of these playful moves a try. You might be surprised by how much joy and closeness they bring to your connection.

In a world that's often rushed and demanding, taking a moment to be playful with your partner can be like a breath of fresh air. It is a reminder that your relationship is a haven of joy, where even the smallest gestures can create ripples of happiness. So, don't be afraid to step out of your comfort zone and infuse your relationship with the spice of playfulness. Your clothes might stay on, but the passion and connection you will feel will be anything but covered up.

5. Learn some new sexual skills and styles

Honestly, keeping things fresh can be pretty exciting. In life, it is the newness that keeps us hooked and interested. The same goes for your intimate moments with your husband. If you want to light up his world and have him eagerly looking forward to those moments of intimacy, you need to add a little spark to your bed skills.

We are not saying you need to become a contortionist or anything, but being a little adventurous in the bedroom can go a long way. Think about it this way: variety is like the secret ingredient that makes sex way more enjoyable. It is like sprinkling that extra dash of excitement into your love life. Don't be shy to try out new things—new ways, new moves, new styles. It is not just about doing it differently for the sake of it; it is about discovering what brings both of you pleasure.

Speaking of pleasure, do not forget the power of foreplay. It is like the appetiser that gets you both hungry for the main course. So, why not put some energy into it? Make it a fun game of teasing, exploring, and discovering each other's erogenous zones. Trust me, this can set the stage for an incredible experience between the sheets.

There's more to it than just physical moves. It is about understanding what truly turns your husband on. There is a whole world of pleasure beyond just the act itself. It is about knowing how to ignite that fire in his mind and body. Communication is your best friend here. Don't be afraid to ask him about his fantasies, his desires, and what gets him going. Remember, great love-making is like a symphony of emotional and physical connections.

Sometimes suggesting new things in the bedroom might feel a bit awkward. But you know what is not awkward? Having an amazing time with your husband and building a stronger connection. It is all about making your marriage a space where you can explore and enjoy each other fully.

"Wake up, North Wind, get moving, South Wind! Breathe on my garden, fill the air with spice fragrance. Oh, let my lover enter his garden! Yes, let him eat the fine, ripe fruits." SOS 4:16 (The Message bible).

5 Ways to Sexually Please Your Wife As A Husband.

1. ***Take your time with foreplay, especially before diving into the main event of sex.*** Remember, when it comes to getting intimate, it is not just about the act of penetration. There is a whole bunch of stuff that builds up to that moment, especially for women. So, if you are aiming to be a true champ at satisfying your partner, patience is your secret weapon during both foreplay and the outcome of the main event.

A good number of women don't react to sensual touches the same way men do. For them, lovemaking works on a different clock. They need more than just a quick switch to get in the mood; their bodies and hormones appreciate a slower and gentle approach, which is why they need more time to have an intimate conversation with their hormones before things get rolling. This is where foreplay comes in. It is not merely a "nice to have," it is like the warm-up before the big game.

Giving your partner that extra attention and time helps set the stage for a truly satisfying experience. It is not about the physical stuff; it is about getting your partner's mind and body in sync with yours. Take it slow, enjoy the foreplay, and ensure your partner is fully on board before you hit the accelerator.

In a nutshell, patience is the name of the game. Think of it like preparing a pot of Smoky Jollof Rice – you don't rush the cooking process. You patiently go through every necessary phase before the meal is ready. After the meal has gone through its due process, you sit, relax and let your taste buds savour your meal. The same goes for the journey to a fulfilling intimate connection. Take your time to build up the anticipation, create a comfortable space, and make sure you are both ready for the ride. Remember, it is not about the destination; the journey is where the magic truly happens.

2. *Become the student of your wife.* Study her moans, moods, and moves. Embracing the role of a student in the realm of intimate connection can be a game-changer in understanding and fulfilling your wife's desires. Consider this: you are about to embark on a fascinating journey of exploration, focusing not on textbooks, but on her—your partner, your lover, your wife. Pay attention to the subtleties that often speak louder than words. Many women are not always vocal about their desires, so it is up to you to be attentive.

Begin with the canvas of her expressions—the windows

to her satisfaction. Her eyes, her mouth, the rhythm of her body—these are the notes composing a symphony of pleasure. Think of it as a beautiful puzzle; each piece of her expression forms a clue, guiding you towards the masterpiece of her pleasure.

Communication is key. It is perfectly alright to have an open conversation about what ignites her desires. And here is a little secret: what tantalises her today might not elicit the same reaction tomorrow. But here is the silver lining: over time, you will create a treasure trove of knowledge about her preferences. You will gradually piece together the mosaic of touches, the symphony of foreplay that orchestrates her ecstasy.

Speaking of foreplay, imagine it as a delicate dance—a dance of tender touches. Picture a feather gently caressing her skin. Softness is your watchword. Begin by delving into her erogenous zones. These are the secret gardens of pleasure, waiting to be discovered. Start with her earlobes and travel slowly to her neck, the gateway to sensation. Then, let your touch journey to her breasts, the nipples—gauge her response. The clitoris, the vulva, the realm of anticipation—it is like creating a roadmap to her satisfaction.

3. **Remember the subtle art of withdrawal.** This dance

involves a rhythm of touch and withdrawal, much like a beautiful suspense in a story. Build it up, then retreat with your touch, letting anticipation linger. This push and pull, this ebb and flow, is the path to ignite her desire. As with any craft, practice refines your skill. Let her guide you; let her cues lead your movements.

4. **Attention to detail matters.** Keep your nails well-tended; gentleness is the rule. These erogenous zones are delicate, deserving of your care. Cleanliness is non-negotiable. Ensure your hands and mouth are clean, safeguarding her from unwanted germs. If your bare hands are in play, remember to wash thoroughly to avoid discomfort—a prickling sensation that could mar a beautiful experience.

Ultimately, becoming a connoisseur of your wife's pleasure is not just a task; it is a privilege. It is a journey that binds you closer, that lets you traverse the landscape of passion hand in hand. It is a testament to your commitment, a silent whisper of your devotion to unlocking the symphony of her desires. And remember, it takes two to tango. While you are deciphering her codes, let her explore yours. In unity, in curiosity, in care, lies the magic of intimate connection—an exquisite dance you are now a part of.

5. **Communicate with kind, appreciative, and sweet**

words that elicit your affection and attention to her emotional needs.

Words have this amazing way of making a big impact, especially on women. When you're getting close and cosy, remember to use kind, appreciative, and sweet words. These words aren't just words; they are like a secret recipe to tap into her emotions and show her that you really care.

Imagine this: as you are sharing those intimate moments, whisper those beautiful words that make her heart skip a beat. It is not just about the physical activities; it is about connecting emotionally too. Whether you are caressing her or taking things further, those words create a magical link that makes her feel like the queen of your world. These simple words hold the power to make her feel loved and cherished, like she is on cloud nine wrapped up in your arms. Almost every woman out there craves this special connection with her partner when in a private space together.

Don't underestimate the power of your words. They are not just sounds; they are the key to unlocking her emotions and making her feel like the most important person in your universe. It is a small effort that can create a big impact on your connection.

Ever thought about timing things just right to make sure she's having a great time in bed? It is all about discovering when she's about to climax, reaching that amazing point of pleasure. Once you have that down, here is a little trick: go for gentle thrusts in and out while making sure you are not reaching your own peak too soon.

This might sound like some kind of secret move, but trust me, it's not about magic—it is about mastering a skill. And like any skill worth having, it takes practice, patience, and some effort. It is like learning to play a musical instrument; you start with the basics and gradually get better as you go along.

It is not just about physical satisfaction; it is about building a deep connection and understanding with your partner. When you are attentive to her pleasure, it shows that you care about her experience and you are willing to put in the effort to make things amazing for both of you.

Remember, this is not a race to the finish line. It is about both of you enjoying the journey. And yes, it might mean holding back a bit to make sure she is getting there first. It might require some sacrifice on your part but the rewards are totally worth it.

Embrace the learning process. Communicate with your partner, pay attention to her cues, and be patient with yourself.

Why some men & women don't enjoy sex

05

As we wrap up this book on the basic elements of sex in marriage, we would like to talk about reasons why some married men and women are asexual (have no sexual feelings or desires for their spouse). The truth is, any child of God who is married is not expected to condescend to the level of asexuality. The reason being that sex is an obligation of couples in a marriage.

However, some individuals may not want or enjoy sex in marriage due to the fact that they have been asexual for a period of time without paying attention to their low sexual libido. And a number of reasons account for this.

Why Some Wives May Not Want or Enjoy Sex In Their Marriage

Personality types: There are certain personality types who might not have a high sexual drive. The Fighter Jet, generally known as the choleric, and the Private Jet known as the Melancholies are less likely to make sexual advancement compared to the Passenger Plane wife who is known as the sanguine.

Those ones are naturally playful and confident, so flirting with their husbands is quite pleasurable for them, especially when they do not have a cultural view about how wives should behave during intercourse.

The last personality which is the Cargo plane, is generally known as the Phlegmatics. These ones are quite sensual in nature, just like the passenger planes, but may rarely make advances.

Childhood Sexual Trauma: A woman may become asexual if she has experienced sexual abuse or near abuse as a child and has been hunted by the memory for a long period of time. This is very possible, especially if she has not found closure through prayers, counselling and therapy.

Often, our culture sweeps such occurrences under the carpet, and they eventually become monsters that could hunt generationally. The definition of trapped trauma leading to therapy is what the Apostle Paul wrote below: *"What I don't understand about myself is that I decide one way, but then I act another way, doing things I absolutely despise. So if I can't be trusted to figure out what is best for myself and then do it, it becomes obvious that God's command is necessary. But I need something more! For if I know the law but still can't keep it, and if the power of sin within me keeps sabotaging my best intentions, I obviously need help!" Romans 7:15–17 (The Message Bible)*

We had an encounter with a young couple. Their marriage was about hitting the rock and it was said to be a spiritual battle. There is a sexual posture, and whenever the husband tries to meet with her in that style, she becomes violent. It was during one of the counselling sessions that it dawned on him that it was a result of a childhood trauma.

Her uncle repeatedly raped her in that position when she lost her dad. Unknown to her husband, that particular style was a bad memory that she never healed from, as it was brushed aside even though her parents knew about it. Nothing was done because of financial help coming from that same man. She endured it for years, and it became her trauma until she sought help.

Previous Betrayal: This occurs when a woman must have had several relationship disappointments before her eventual marriage, especially when sex was involved. The woman has to realise that old things have passed away and she is with her husband. Her husband is not the one she fornicated with or who hurt her badly. She needs to detoxify her emotions.

Products of Circumcision: It takes a sexually skilled and patient husband to lead a wife in this category to pleasurable sex that will make them climax. The reason is that the clitoris was cut off during circumcision. According to Bonobology.com, December 15, 2022, research suggests clitoral stimulation is what turns women on the most, even more than vaginal penetration. Circumcision is not a sexual death sentence. There are ways that she can still get aroused around her clitoris and other parts of her erogenous zones.

Pregnancy or menopause: This is another reason why some women tend to have a distaste for sex. The significant change in their physiology during these stages of life makes the act of sex unappealing to them. But with proper orientation, mindset, and medical intervention where necessary, wives experiencing this phase of their lives can get help and still enjoy sex maximally.

Health challenge: The Preacher talked about the time to embrace and the time to refrain from embracing (Ecclesiastes 3:5). When life happens in this dimension, particularly when it's a serious health challenge, little or nothing can be done sexually. That's why, as beautiful as sexual pleasure is, it's not all we do in marriage. May everyone with a relatable challenge such as this receive grace in Jesus name.

Many years ago, a pastor's wife approached us to seek counsel. Her husband suddenly developed an erection problem. They had both been faithful to each other and had enjoyed a beautiful sexual life. It was becoming a burden for them, as they had both been sexually starved for over a year. We advised that they become more skilled in their foreplay to still enjoy orgasm and the pleasure of having each other.

Stress: This is a common factor in our ever-busy world today. It is more pertinent to critically pay more attention to wives in marriages of African orientation where the husbands are not raised to carry out house chores. When a woman is tired from the day's work or business and is also solely responsible for taking care of the home with little or no assistance from her husband, sex becomes an additional duty to be carried out. Then she gets disturbed about the fact that the little strength she has left is being demanded by her husband through sexual advances. In that instance, she sees such a move as stress rather than sex as a stress reliever.

Religious orientation: Some religious doctrines forbid women to make sexual advances. As long as your sexual lives as a couple do not negatively affect your spiritual and physical health, whatever a couple chooses to do is within their marital life and marital bed. Ensure you stay away from any appearance of sexual disorder. Be that wife who looks forward to satisfying her husband in bed even as you make up your mind to rid yourself of religious barriers that are based on personal biases. 1 Corinthians 7:2, (The Message Bible)- "Sexual drives are strong, but marriage is strong enough to contain them and provide for a balanced and fulfilling sexual life in a world of sexual disorder."

Traditional mindset about sex: There are traditions that believe that it is taboo for women to be open about sexual advances towards their husbands. Some husbands are also not comfortable with their wives demanding sex. This is not the Kingdom standard. Your bodies are meant for each other. The scriptures say: *"The wife does not have authority over her own body, but the husband does. And* *likewise, the husband does not have authority over his own body, but the wife does."*1 Corinthians 7:4.

Low self-esteem: Some wives are not confident and proud of themselves because they probably have low self-esteem issues. Some were body-shamed growing up. Life might have happened to some either through accident, childbirth, or a health challenge. Whatever it is, look at yourself in the mirror and let your scars be a reminder of what you have received through the storm of life. With your head up, be determined to be sensual in your marriage and enjoy sex in marriage with your legal spouse.

Why Some Husbands May Not Want or Enjoy Sex In Their Marriage

1. Fear of not meeting sexual expectations: Your husband could shy away from sex if he is not sure of meeting your sexual satisfaction. Anxiety may set in when this feeling becomes consistent, especially when it has to do with sexual dysfunction. Medical conditions such as erectile dysfunction, premature ejaculation, and delayed ejaculation can make sex embarrassing or strike a blow to your husband's sexual confidence.

2. *Ageing:* This is a reality that the majority of men must be prepared to live with. This can also contribute to concerns about declining performance or declining physical appeal which can affect confidence in the bedroom. Men who have early prostate cancer may find this really challenging when talking about engaging in regular sex.

3. *Personality type:* Just as personality affects the sexual performance of women, it also influences men. There are personalities who, by default, could have a low libido especially when they are passing through challenges or are busy with other aspects of their lives.

The Fighter Jets, also called the Cholerics are more of goal-getters than fun lovers. They may not think about sex during the busy period of their lives. Once their mind is on a particular project, everything else ceases to exist unless they become intentional about their work-life balance. Looking at a passenger plane, otherwise called the Sanguine, when stressed or overly engaged with certain goals, he is likely to see sex as a calmer and what he needs.

4. *Unexpected or lingering stress:* When you are experiencing heavy stress, everyday joys start to lose their appeal. Food doesn't taste as good, your favourite

TV show doesn't make you laugh as much, and you may even deny yourself pleasure because you feel you're not worthy. Stressors outside the bedroom, such as work stress, money concerns, fatigue, and depression, can affect a man's sexual interests. Nonetheless, a Christian man must be in charge so that additional stress does not come from a constantly dissatisfied wife in the bedroom.

5. Resentful and Domineering Wife: Often, a man may become asexual towards a wife who shows resentment and domineering tendencies. No man likes to be controlled, especially by a woman like his wife. So whenever a man observes this attitude in his wife, he begins to withdraw from her, even sexually.

6. Extramarital affairs: Men who cheat on their wives or masturbate regularly hardly look forward to sex in marriage. Because their sexual attention has been divided and due to the fact that they probably enjoy a better kind of sexual pleasure outside their marriage bed with sinful partners or through pornography. The problem with this is that, sometimes, this unhealthy disposition forces some women into cheating as well. However, this kind of thing should never be found among the kingdom-minded husbands and wives.

WRAPPING IT UP

As we come to the end of this enlightening journey through "The ABC of Intentional Sex in Marriage," we hope you've discovered that the essence of physical intimacy goes far beyond the physical act itself.

Remember that our intention in sharing these insights was not merely to enhance your bedroom experiences, but to enrich your entire married life. The wisdom you've gained within these pages is meant to infuse your marriage with renewed passion, understanding, and a deeper bond.

As you move forward, keep in mind that the principles and practices shared here can be your compass, guiding you through the ever-changing terrain of marriage.

We pray that your love continue to flourish and your connection with your spouse deepens with each passing day. May you remain steadfast in your commitment to fostering a God-given, people-centered union that not only elevates your marriage but also shines as an example for others to follow.

We encourage you to hold onto the valuable lessons you've learned and allow them to shape your journey ahead. Remember that your marriage is unique, and it is your intentionality, authenticity, and dedication that will ensure it remains a remarkable and enduring tale.

Thank you for allowing us to be a part of your pursuit of intentional sex in marriage.

We wish you a future filled with unending joy, boundless connection, and an unbreakable bond.

With love and best wishes,
Sola & Nike Ajayi

About the authors

Sola & Nike Ajayi are Certified Family Life Practitioners, Pastors, and and thriving Entrepreneurs. With a wealth of experience and a deep commitment to guiding and nurturing relationships, they stand as pillars of wisdom and support.

Ministry Leadership

Dedicating themselves to spiritual leadership, the couple serves as Pastors responsible for the RCCG Sunshine Assembly Zone. Additionally, they assume the role of coordinating Pastors for the Young Adults and Youth at RCCG, Lagos Province 7. Their leadership extends beyond the spiritual realm as they have ventured into various other areas.

Professional Training and Accreditation

Sola & Nike Ajayi's expertise in Family Life Coaching and Marriage Counseling is a result of rigorous training and accreditation from prestigious institutions. They have been certified by The Institute of Family Engineering &

Development in Nigeria, The Rising Oaks Ministry in Canada, The Institute of Marriage and Family Affairs in the USA, and the RCCG National Family Affairs Unit.

Realm Academy for Family Life

As visionaries behind the REALM ACADEMY FOR FAMILY LIFE, Sola & Nike Ajayi have established a comprehensive platform to cater to diverse aspects of family development. This innovative academy is home to six distinctive groups:

- *Relationship and Marriage Mentors Program:* Offering guidance to couples at every stage of their relationship journey.

- *Personal Progress Program:* Empowering individuals with personal growth tools and strategies.

- *Get Set... Marry:* Providing expert insights for singles on the path to marriage.

- *The Marriage Match Minder:* Assisting couples in building strong and lasting marriages.

- *Cradle ⅖:* Catering to parents in nurturing and raising children.

- *Happily Ever After:* Focusing on sustaining joyful and fulfilling marriages.

Personal Journey

With nearly two decades of marriage, Sola & Nike Ajayi are living examples of the principles they teach. Their union is blessed with three remarkable children who are destined to make a positive impact on the world.

Sola & Nike Ajayi's dedication to fostering healthy relationships, their diverse expertise, and their dynamic leadership have positioned them as significant influencers in the realm of family life and marriage coaching.

www.ingramcontent.com/pod-product-compliance
Lightning Source LLC
Chambersburg PA
CBHW070543160726
48003CB00005B/1857